PARABLES OF THE BARRIO

VOL. 1, NOS. 1 – 50

Other Books by Juan M. Flavier:

Doctor to the Barrios
My Friends in the Barrios
Back to the Barrios

PARABLES OF THE BARRIO

VOL. I, NOS. 1-50

JUAN M. FLAVIER

New Day Publishers

Cover Design: **Florante C. Belardo**

ISBN 971-10-0943-9 (Bp)
ISBN 971-10-0381-3 (Np)

First Impression, 1988
Sixth Impression, 2005

CONTENTS

PREFACE

This book was born in Sri Lanka where I had the pleasure of travelling with my very good friend, A.T. Ariyarante of the world-famous Sarvodaya Shramadana Movement. This movement is the biggest non-governmental rural development organization in any Third World country I know. For a week, we visited together one-third of the whole country which covered 8,000 villages.

As Ari and I travelled, he would propose a topic like cooperation, unity, greed or change, and I was asked to relate a parable on any of them. He would also relate his own stories and we had a lot of fun together.

After some time I realized that I had quite a number of parables. Many of those to whom I related them asked if I had written them down. They invariably encouraged me to get them into print. I promised Ari that I would write them down, and this collection is the fulfillment of that promise.

Some of these parables are my own, many I have read from books, while others I have heard in the barrios. I have used all of them in talks and speeches in the barrios, not only here in the Philippines but also in Sri Lanka, China, Vietnam, Ghana and other countries.

To be effective, a parable must be adapted to the audience and the situation; it must be detailed especially if used for an audience in the barrio, which is always my target. Hence, most of these parables have rural settings.

If some of these parables can be used by others in driving home a point or two, I would feel amply justified in writing them.

As many of my readers know, these parables are being serialized in the *Philippine Star*. For this, I thank Mrs. Betty Go-Belmonte.

I also wish to acknowledge the many nameless people who shared their own stories which are reflected in this book.

Special thanks are due my secretary, Amy de Vega, and the other members of the secretarial pool, who suffered through innumerable drafts.

I acknowledge with great appreciation the support and commitment to our mission of my colleagues in the IIRR (International Institute for Rural Reconstruction).

To my wife and children, I hope this book will make up for all the time I used which was rightfully theirs.

This book is timely in that it coincides with my 25th anniversary in rural reconstruction and the selection of the IIRR as the Ramon Magsaysay Awardee in International Understanding.

JUAN M. FLAVIER

IIRR, Silang, Cavite
Philippines
23 June 1987

1

THE PARABLE OF THE PATRON SAINT

The farmer was an avid devotee of San Isidro, the Patron Saint of farmers and laborers. Every time he had a problem or special petition, he prayed to the patron. Each evening before bedtime and every morning upon rising, he said a special prayer to the saint.

On his way to his farm, it was his daily ritual to drop in at the *kapilya* (chapel) and utter a short prayer, a classical *bisita iglesia,* for it would last no more than a minute. He would make a quick sign of the cross, genuflect and rush out. He was then assured of a blessed day.

The farmer named his first son Isidro in honor of the saint. A medallion of San Isidro was always pinned on his shirt, on the left side of his chest just directly outside his throbbing heart. This he wore at work and wherever he went. He removed the medallion only when he took a bath.

He was not a man of means by any stretch of the imagination. His crops fed the family, and his children attended the barrio school. Though he had very little to spare, all he could set aside was for the fiesta.

On San Isidro's birthday or fiesta, he would gratefully prepare food in honor of his patron saint.

One time, the farmer strolled beyond his farm. This was an area he rarely visited because of a steep ravine. Not knowing the terrain well, he unknowingly moved close to the drop. Suddenly the soil on which he stood caved in and he fell.

Fortunately, his quick reflexes enabled him to clutch on to a fragile vine on the precarious slope. He looked down and felt dizzy. He saw death awaiting him on the sharp and menacing rocks hundreds of feet below.

Instinctively, the farmer called to his patron saint: "San Isidro, please save me. In a second this vine will give way and I will surely die!"

In a flash, a booming voice shattered the stillness from above. "I am San Isidro!"

"I knew you would come to my rescue, O holy San Isidro," exclaimed the farmer, ecstatic with joy. "Please save me." The farmer looked up but could see no one.

"First, do you have faith in me?" asked San Isidro's authoritative voice.

"Yes, yes, patron. You know that I pray to you daily. My son is named after you. In spite of my poverty, I celebrate the fiesta, all because of my undying faith in you."

"Very well then," said San Isidro, "let go of the vine. As you fall down the ravine, I will catch you."

The farmer was silent for a split second, then shouted to the sky, "Anybody else up there?"

2

THE PARABLE OF THE LETTER TO GOD

During the last typhoon, Lencho lost all his rice crop because of a severe flood. The whole barrio was affected so he had no one to turn to for help.

In sheer desperation, Lencho wrote a letter to God:

"Dear God:

The typhoon devastated my whole crop. We have nothing left. I have seven children. Please, God, send me one hundred pesos to tide us over.

Sincerely yours,

Lencho"

He actually placed the letter in an envelope, stuck a stamp on it, and mailed it to "God in Heaven."

The letter reached the post office but it could not be delivered. However, the postmen had the time of their life laughing at the oddity of a man actually writing to God. Some people said God was dead, but here was a farmer writing to God out of sheer faith. The postmen decided to show the odd letter to their postmaster.

"Do you want to laugh today, sir?" the postmen asked their boss.

"Why, yes," answered the postmaster eagerly.

And so the letter was handed to the postmaster who read the letter to God. But he did not laugh. Instead he reread the letter in all seriousness and then faced the postmen.

"We talk of social action," he said. "We all speak of the brotherhood of all men. Yet here is a man in dire need and you think it is funny? Shouldn't we pool our resources instead and help Lencho?"

The postmen were embarrassed by the truth of the postmaster's remarks. So the group decided to pass the hat around and raise money among themselves to assist Lencho.

But they were few and money was difficult to come by, so all the post office personnel could raise was eighty pesos. Nevertheless, that was better than doing nothing.

They also decided to play the game with Lencho, so they placed the money in an envelope, put a stamp complete with stampmark, and wrote on the upper left-hand corner: "From God in Heaven."

A postman personally handcarried the letter with the money to Lencho in the barrio, who was ecstatic with joy. "I knew God would answer my plea," he exclaimed. "God did not forget to send the money!"

Lencho quickly counted the paper bills and found only eighty pesos, instead of the one hundred he had asked for. So he wrote another letter.

"Dear God:

Thank you for answering my prayer, God. But, please, next time, do not send the money through the post office, because the people there are thieves.

Sincerely yours,

Lencho"

3

THE PARABLE OF THE CHURCH SITE

The town was in a frenzy. For years the people had been talking about building a church through their own efforts. Many ways of raising the substantial outlay were devised and painfully implemented. Finally the needed amount was raised to the pleasure and elation of the whole community. Their dream of a church of their own was happily near.

Unexpectedly, a problem arose regarding the site of the structure. No site was available in the center of the town, so the only other possible places were at the edge of town. When the tentative site was in the northern part of town, the barrio people on the southern side objected; the reverse was equally objected to by the other side. Soon the villages in the east and the west areas of town entered the fray and voiced their objection to a church site unduly far from them.

The impasse became irresoluble and the debates grew bitter with time. Their much vaunted unity proved brittle and superficial. The town was in a quandary.

It was in the midst of this dissension that an unforgettable incident occurred.

First, as though to exhibit displeasure over the wrangling among the townspeople, an unusual drought occurred.

The heat wave further aggravated the cracked soil. The hot air seared the rice crop at the all-crucial time of fruiting.

When harvest time came, the people's worst fears came to pass. Whereas in previous years, the average yield was ninety cavans per hectare, that year the harvest did not go beyond five cavans per hectare. There was talk of hunger for the first time in living memory.

Two of the farmers who were the best of friends met the same fate. Both were rice growers in adjacent barrios of the town. Since their land had poor soil, the reduction in their yield was even more devastating. Both harvested only one cavan in their respective less-than-a hectare rice farms. Both farmers were very much worried about the welfare of their families and their friends.

One night, the first farmer thought of his friend in the adjacent barrio. They may have nothing to eat now, he said to himself. So he did something beautiful. He divided his yield of one cavan into two shares. In the darkness of the night, he carried the half sack of rice on his shoulders. Carefully, he trudged through the pathway leading to the next barrio to deliver his gift of love.

At exactly the same time, the second farmer had the same thought. He was concerned for his friend and his family's sustenance. He also divided his yield and carried the half sack on his shoulders. In the pitch darkness, he hiked toward the adjacent barrio to deliver his brotherly gift.

At the border between the two barrios, the two friends practically bumped into each other.

"Where are you going at this time of the night?" asked the first farmer.

"To your home to give you this half sack of rice," answered the second farmer. "And you?"

The first farmer could not help laughing as he put down his load. "I was on my way to give you this half sack of rice as your share of my poor harvest."

The two best friends embraced in the darkness as they exchanged their half sacks of rice. No words were needed, as tears welled from their eyes.

At the exact place where these two best friends met that blessed night, the town decided to build their church. Putting aside their previous disagreements, they all believed that the site was the point nearest to heaven.

4

THE PARABLE OF THE CREATION (Part I)

In the biblical version, God created man and woman in their full form. In this barrio version, God created the human body part by part. One day, He created all kinds of heads—big heads and small ones, dull heads and bright ones, round heads and square ones, hairy heads and even bald ones.

Next, God created all sorts of necks, then bodies—plump shapes and narrow ones, curved shapes and bulging ones.

The following day, He created arms, legs, feet and all the other parts.

He then lined up the human parts in a wide field. When everything was ready, He called out for everyone to select the kind of body parts each fancied and desired.

Those who responded early got choice parts—good heads, well-formed necks, shapely bodies, and well-proportioned extremities. The laggards got all the left-overs.

The story goes that when God made the call, the first to respond were the westerners, so they got the prominent and high-bridged (*matangos*) noses.

The next group that heeded the announcement were the other Asians. So they got the next best noses—not too prominent but quite well-formed.

The last to respond were the Filipinos who got only the left-over flat noses (*pango*).

The sequel has God creating man and woman by baking. He mixed the best wheat flour available and added the freshest water from the spring of life.

The head was formed together with the ears and imprints of the eyes, nose and mouth. The right proportion of torso and well-extended extremities, toes and fingers, were carefully shaped.

When all was perfect, God lovingly placed the dough in the oven with just the right heat. After some time, He pulled out the tray and pressed His finger on the belly. The impression formed the belly button (navel or *pusod*). It was not yet fully cooked and the form was whitish. Those humans became the Caucasians.

God repeated the whole process and again cooked the form in the oven. He wanted to make sure it was well cooked. When the figure was retrieved, it was burned. These became the black race found in the African region.

This time God wanted it just right. He baked another set and placed it in the oven, remembering that the first was undercooked and produced white forms, and the second was overcooked and produced the blacks.

So God made sure the baking time was just right. Thus, when

He pulled out the third form from the oven, the color was perfect. It was golden brown! Thus was created the Filipinos with their enviable tan.

5

THE PARABLE OF THE CREATION (Part II)

God created the world including man and woman. People had been assigned to their respective lands. What remained was the allocation of scarce natural resources.

God was methodical and purposive. His voice boomed with authority. "Sugar for Cuba, and some sugar for the Philippines. Gold for Ghana, and some gold for the Philippines. Coconuts for Sri Lanka, and some coconuts for the Philippines. Sunshine for Hawaii and some sunshine for the Philippines. Oil for Saudi Arabia and some oil for the Philippines. Rice for Thailand and some rice for the Philippines. Bananas for Nicaragua and some bananas for the Philippines." At this point the grumbling became loud and recriminatory.

"But, God," complained one country respectfully, "it seems unfair that the Philippines gets some of what all the others are given."

God was unperturbed and even showed the beginnings of a smile. His voice remained firm and booming. "Don't feel bad," He announced, "I am also giving them the Spaniards, the Japanese and the Americans."

The allocation of natural resources under the dominion of mankind had been completed. God was pleased with the results.

The people of the world were equally gratified at the bounty of God's blessings. All the resources needed were in place: plants on land and fishes in the sea, birds in the air, and the proper climate spread over the globe.

Man's spokesman stood up and addressed God: "In the name of the people all over the world, we thank you most sincerely. You have provided for our needs now and for the long future. We pray for guidance that we may be good stewards of these treasures."

God nodded His head knowingly.

A second speaker rose and declared: "God, we truly thank you for all your blessings. But while you are at it, could you please give each country a good government? This way we can be ruled with justice, equity and decency."

God was composed and did not look surprised. In fact, he looked as if He had expected the special request.

Then He spoke. "Resources I can give you. But a good government? Ah, that you have to evolve yourself. A good government is not a gift from God. It is an achievement of the people."

6

THE PARABLE OF HELL

The farmer had just passed away and was sent directly to hell. St. Peter stood at the gate to check his name and lead him on a tour of hell. It was more interesting than the farmer had expected. His stereotyped idea of hell as a huge hole of fire was not accurate.

What he saw was a series of many holes. The classification was based on nationality, arranged alphabetically: Argentina, Brazil, Chile, and so on, one hole per country.

The holes were deep and emitted heat. Screaming voices could be heard everywhere. Each hole was tightly covered by strong iron bars to prevent anybody from escaping.

Eagerly he looked for the Philippine hole. And there it was—after Paraguay. But, how strange! The Philippine section was unique because it had no iron bars nor any other form of cover.

"St. Peter," he said, "the Filipinos in hell must be in a good-conduct hole. I notice there is no cover. Why is that?"

St. Peter's face was expressionless as he answered, "Oh, the

Filipinos are no problem. For them, there is no need for any cover. You see, every time a Filipino succeeds in climbing near the top, the others below pull him down."

As part of the tour in hell, he was shown the eating premises. The first dining hall looked typical—nothing unusual. There were long tables with built-in seats more like long benches anchored to the table legs.

"Nothing remarkable here," he reacted to St. Peter's comments.

"Note the spoons and forks," St. Peter pointed out. "Notice how long they are?"

He strained his eyes and remarked in surprise, "Why, yes, the eating utensils are three feet long and are connected permanently to their arms. No wonder the people are so thin; they cannot get the food to their own mouths."

The next dining hall was exactly like the first, with long tables and benches. Even the spoons and forks were equally long—three feet long and also permanently anchored to their arms. However, the people here were strikingly different! They were all in excellent health—all were robust and looked properly nourished.

"How can that be when there seems to be no difference in the facilities?" the farmer asked, looking at St. Peter wonderingly.

Instead of explaining, St. Peter directed his attention to how they ate. There it was! Each did not extend his three-foot spoon and fork to himself, but fed the person directly in front of him. Meanwhile, the opposite man fed the one who extended the food to him.

The power of sharing at its best!

7

THE PARABLE OF THE GATE TO HEAVEN

A landlord, a rich merchant, and a farmer passed away at about the same time. The three ascended to the gates of heaven for the final entry.

St. Peter waited by the outer gate to process the new arrivals.

Being unfamiliar with formalities and interviews, the farmer was gripped with fear and uncertainty. He did not even know whether he was destined for heaven or for hell. He became particularly apprehensive when St. Peter began to shoot questions as each stood in front of him in apparent judgment. Depending on the answer, the person was either admitted to heaven or sent to another stairs leading downwards. The farmer suspected that the descent led to the ports of hell.

The farmer trembled uncontrollably. As his turn came nearer, he overheard the question of St. Peter. The question was standard and the same for everyone. And so simple.

"Do I hear the question correctly?" the farmer asked an angel helping in maintaining order among the people in the line.

"Yes, it is a simple spelling test," the angel assured him. "The same word is asked because here everyone is equal. Not only that, I think St. Peter really wants everybody to enter the gates of heaven."

And so it was, indeed. The farmer breathed a sigh of relief.

A tenant was now facing St. Peter. "Spell GOD," asked the good Saint in a drawling monotonous voice.

"G-O-D," answered the tenant hurriedly.

"Correct. Go in to heaven," said St. Peter without the slightest change in expression. "Next, please."

Then the rich merchant quickly moved forward. The question was the same. "Spell GOD," St. Peter intoned mechanically.

"G-O-D," responded the enthusiastic rich merchant rapidly lest the word be changed.

"Good. Enter heaven."

Then came the farmer's turn. By now, he was composed and self-assured. He could spell that word!

St. Peter looked at the farmer and slowly said, "Spell the word ECCLESIASTICAL."

8

THE PARABLE OF THE BODY PARTS

The farmer entered the heavenly realm with caution and eagerness. He was curious to see for the first time what the place and the people looked like. For on earth, his own vision of heaven and the expectations of others varied. Some said in heaven people were but silhouettes walking on clouds. Others spoke of a dull monotony with everyone in robes of white playing the lyre while some had wings and halos.

As he tiptoed in, the sight of the people shocked him. They had grotesque and disfigured shapes. Only certain parts of their body remained. None had the complete human forms he had known down on earth.

He asked an angel passing by, "Is this hell where I landed?"

"No. This is the life beyond," answered the angel.

"But why are the people so mangled?" the farmer pursued.

"If you look closely, you will see that each one has only a part of his original body," explained the angel. "For the rule in heaven dictates that you retain the part of your body you used most and lose the parts you least employed. That man over there," the angel pointed to a pair of standing legs, "was a long-distance runner. All that remains are his racing feet."

The farmer surveyed the surroundings. It was true—he saw only body parts.

There was the politician. He only had his big mouth and thick lips left. True to form, he continued to blabber and harangue the people around him.

In a corner was a driver. His hands, gnarled and calloused, still clenched as though clutching a steering wheel. He was alternately cheerful and grouchy.

A scientist had only his brains floating in the air. Unmindful of the world around him, he still thought of equations and theories.

A government clerk had only his buttocks, uselessly sitting on his squeaking chair and drunk with his rude sense of importance.

A pair of knees turned out to be a religious. He kept praying for the salvation of mankind, petitioning for the poor who were getting poorer each day.

A stevedore had his bulky shoulder, ready to carry every

imaginable load.

At the center of the spacious area was a big heart, beating with life and feeling. The farmer could not guess whose it was.

"Whose is that huge and expansive heart?" he asked an angel.

The angel looked at him and answered with pride and admiration,

"That belongs to the Rural Reconstruction Worker!"

9

THE PARABLE OF THE PROFESSIONALS

As was his habit, St. Peter sat at the entrance of heaven. He liked to interview each arrival from earthly life. He was particularly interested in knowing what the person had done for a living. This would give him an idea of good deeds done as a basis for deciding whether to allow him entrance or to remand him to the lower section where flames burned all day long.

The new batch consisted mostly of professionals. The first man approached St. Peter with confidence.

"What did you do on earth? And why should I accept you into heaven?" asked St. Peter.

"I was a doctor. I attended to the sick and the wounded. I also prevented diseases by making people healthy through immunization and other public health measures. I always responded to the call of the people."

"Enter heaven," St. Peter intoned solemnly. "Next, please. What did you do on earth, and why should I accept you into heaven?"

"I was a lawyer and I defended the accused and the condemned. I was a guardian of truth and a champion of law and order. I guided and counseled people to settle disputes. I was always at the service of the people."

"Proceed to the gate," the Saint commanded. "Next, please. What did you do on earth? Why should I accept you into heaven?"

"I was an engineer on earth. I constructed houses for people to live in. I built skyscrapers for offices and other needs of the people. I spanned rivers by constructing bridges. Man has made advances through my endeavors. I was always an active partner in the progress of the people."

"Go past the gates into heaven. Next, please," said St. Peter.

"And what have you to say for yourself?"

"I was a teacher, and I taught all of them."

"Enter heaven. And, in addition, here is a halo and a pair of wings," said St. Peter to the elated teacher.

10

THE PARABLE OF THE LOVER

The man was a most conscientious farmer. His ricefield was located three kilometers away from his home. To save time, he would bring along his noon meal, and this meant being away the whole day.

This he did by choice as he wanted to provide for his family. Day in and day out, he labored in the fields.

One day, a friend informed him about a mysterious man who consorted with his wife in his absence during the day. He inquired discreetly from his neighbors, but no one could be specific. All they could tell him was that the daily visitor smoked a cigar.

Finally, he decided to surprise his wife and her lover by going home at mid-morning.

True enough, the wife was taken aback by his sudden appearance. But the lover was able to hide and could not be seen anywhere.

"I know he is here," the farmer shouted. "Where is he? I can smell cigar smoke. He must be here."

The suspicious and furious husband looked everywhere, but could not locate the lover. He then looked out of the window and saw a man passing by smoking a cigar.

"Aha, there you are," he blurted. Thereupon, he lifted the heavy *baul* (foot locker) and flung it at the suspected culprit.

The scene changed to the heavenly domain of St. Peter. He sat behind a table on which was a huge book containing names of future arrivals.

Three men stood before him ready for their final interview. The first one was asked what led to his journey to heaven.

"You see, St. Peter, I was so angry I lifted a heavy baul and threw it out of the window," he explained. "Under the strain of lifting the baul, my chest constricted with a sudden pain. I must have had a heart attack—the last thing I remember was dropping to the floor and passing out. So here I am."

"I see," commented St. Peter. "Go inside. Your name is on the list."

The second man moved forward and answered, "I was walking along the road minding my own business and enjoying my cigar when suddenly a baul hit me very hard. I think my head and my whole body were crushed by the impact—so here I am."

"Yes, I heard you," St. Peter remarked. "Get in. Your name is also on the list."

Then the third man approached and said, "St. Peter, I was inside the baul smoking my cigar when suddenly I felt someone lift the baul and throw it out of the window!"

11

THE PARABLE OF THE CATFISH

Pedrito and Jose were inseparable friends in their early teens. The barrio called them *kambal* (twins) because wherever one was, the other was invariably there, too.

They were neighbors so they were together from early morning till deep into the night. Oftentimes, they slept in each other's house. Being of the same age, they were classmates in the barrio school. They even had plans to attend first year high school in town together.

It was only natural that on Sundays, Pedrito and Jose went

together to church in town. They wore their Sunday best (*maong*, t-shirt and rubber shoes) even if they took a shortcut through the ricefields.

Taking the regular road, the distance to town would be seven kilometers. By traversing a more direct route behind the cluster of huts and using the rice paddy dikes, the distance was shortened by half. This was called *pagtawid* as it involved crossing a stretch of ricefields and bamboo groves as well as a rivulet.

In one of their pagtawid, on their way to church, they saw a *putikan* (mud puddle) or a *lubluban* (carabao's wallowing hole) in the middle of a deserted field. The hole was teeming with *hito* (fresh water catfish). Either someone used it as a stocking area to increase the weight of the catfish or the farmers missed out because the putikan was out of the usual pathway.

Meeting such an opportunity, one would gather the catch. Ideally the two boys should go to church first and then retrieve the catch on the way back. The problem was that someone else might discover and harvest the fish while they were in church.

Finally, they thought of a solution calling for their rare separation. Pedrito would stay, catch all the fish, go home to the barrio and divide the harvest between them. Jose would proceed to town, attend church and pray for the two of them. They would then have the best of both worlds.

So Pedrito removed his shoes and Sunday pants and caught all the fish. He then fashioned a reed and secured each fish through the gills for easy transport. In the barrio, Pedrito dutifully divided the catch equally according to number and even size. *Hating kapatid* is the barrio term, signifying equitable division or even erring to the advantage of the other.

Meanwhile, Jose heard mass and prayed for the two of them. But while in church, he kept wondering whether Pedrito would really divide the fish equitably, even suspecting that Pedrito might try to claim the bigger ones and give him the smaller fish only.

The question is raised: who is more religious, Pedrito who was not able to go to church but was just in his actuations, or Jose who heard mass but suspected ill-will?

THE PARABLE OF THE FISHERMAN

The fisherman was a great devotee of San Antonio, the patron saint of those who make a living by fishing.

Every day before the fisherman went to the lake, he prayed to the saint for a good catch. An image of the saint was perched on a ledge above his door, so he never missed the special petition before going down the bamboo stairs.

In his bedroom, the fisherman had a huge picture, cut from an old calendar, of his patron saint. Every night, he would pray to this picture before retiring and in the morning before arising.

That day, the fisherman completed his whole prayer ritual. He implored the saint to provide a bountiful catch. With great expectations, he picked up his fishing rod, line, sinker, hook and bait. To confirm his great faith in the Patron, he brought along a big fish basket for the day's catch.

For hours, the fisherman waited patiently for a bite, but in vain. It was as though all the fish had suddenly gone elsewhere. So, finally, he decided to repeat his petition. He looked up to the clear sky and reverently uttered, "San Antonio, please help me to catch some fish. If you do, I solemnly promise to give you the first fish I get today."

As if in direct answer to his prayer, he felt a strong tug on the line. The cork float sank and a vigorous splash confirmed the bite of a two-foot beauty.

The fisherman carefully placed the huge fish on the ground and slowly disentangled the hook from its mouth.

Greed shone in the man's eyes as he said to himself, "What a nice succulent fish. I will take it for myself. To hell with San Antonio. He doesn't need the fish anyway."

He had barely completed the sentence when in a flash the fish jumped back into the lake, where it instantly disappeared among the grass reeds.

The fisherman glanced up to the sky and quickly said, "San Antonio, *hindi ka na mabiro?*" ("Saint Anthony, can't you even take a joke?")

THE PARABLE OF THE OPTIONS

The farmer was getting sick and tired of making choices. Yet, at every turn, he found the necessity of choosing one way or another. He tried to avoid it, but the need to decide kept cropping up. It seemed that every situation presented an exasperating set of options and he just had to select and decide.

For the baptism of his son, the church deacon asked, "First class or second class?"

The farmer visited the cemetery; there the caretaker asked him, "South or North Cemetery?"

He went to see a movie and the *takilyera* (ticket dispenser) asked, "Orchestra or balcony?"

He went to bet at the *sabung* to avoid all the hustle. The *Kristo* (bet-taker or matchmaker) said, "*Sa pula o sa puti?*" ("On the red or the white rooster?")

All he needed was a kilo of salt. The vendor wanted to know, "*Pino o magaspang?*" ("Fine granules or rock salt?")

Even the simple act of ordering beverage involved a complicated set of choices.

"Coffee or tea?" asked the waiter in the restaurant.

"Tea," the farmer answered.

"Chinese or Ceylon tea?"

"Ceylon."

"With kalamansi or milk?"

"With kalamansi," replied the farmer resignedly.

Then the farmer bought some cigarettes and he was confronted with another set of selections:

"King size or regular?"

"Filtered or unfiltered?"

"Mentholated or not?"

"Flip top box or ordinary?"

One day, the farmer accidentally fell into a deep ravine. Fortunately, he was able to grab a protruding branch. Precariously, he held on.

"Help," he shouted. "Somebody, please help me." But no one

answered.

Finally, in sheer desperation, he looked up and pleaded with his patron saint: "St. Francis, please help me."

A voice from the sky asked, "Which St. Francis? St. Francis of Assisi? St. Francis Xavier? or St. Francis de Sales?"

14

THE PARABLE OF SUMMER

A group of farmers huddled under the spreading branches of a huge mango tree. Two sat on the protruding root. The others squatted on the ground.

It was a fair season. Their rice yield equalled that of the previous year. There was nothing to complain about, but they were dreaming of what could be if more water were available.

The barrio did not have irrigation; they relied solely on the natural rainfall starting June of every year. Consequently, they only had one crop per season. During the dry summer spell, they could grow no rice or vegetables.

"What would happen if we could abolish summer?" asked a farmer.

"Why, we could have a second crop," replied another.

The others listened thoughtfully. "Even a secondary crop of vegetables would really be something."

They took turns considering what that would mean—more crops and added income. As the discussion progressed, exaggerations became more and more humorous.

"That is all a very nice dream," an old man brought them back to reality. "But how can we get rid of summer?"

"Well, let us ask God," suggested a young farmer. "Only He can do that."

They unanimously decided to implore God. "We have nothing to lose. If God does not agree, we still have what we have now. But suppose He agrees?"

The thought kept them excited. So they went to God with their special petition to abolish summer.

And it came to pass that God granted the farmers their wish. They couldn't believe it, but the verdict was clear: from then on, no more summers. Plenty of rain and opportunities for more crops.

Eagerly, the farmers prepared their fields. They could now farm the whole year round. In two years they planted five crops of rice. In between they had all sorts of vegetables. They described the situation as the arrival of paradise. Incomes rose three-fold. Prosperity and progress were in the air.

In the third year, however, there came the price to pay. The fields were attacked by a horde of insects never seen before. Ricefields were devastated and vegetables were devoured by the endless swarm of small creatures.

The farmers remembered God. "Let us ask God what happened. We requested for no summer, but not for this calamity. What is going on? Just when we are about to see our dream fulfilled! Why, God?"

And God spoke: "You asked for the abolition of summer to have dryness. Without moisture the insects die and are naturally controlled. So, now, decide what you really want—more yield or less insects?"

The farmers bowed their heads. "God, give us back the original pattern—the orderly design of alternating summer and rainy season. You know best, God."

And so it came to pass that the alternate seasons of drought and wetness returned to earth.

15

THE PARABLE OF THE PRIEST

The parish priest was new in the rural town, having arrived less than a week before. It was also his first assignment and he did not know the people nor the whereabouts of the place. He had been to the plaza (adjoining the church), the market not too far off and to a few homes of the nearby parishioners.

It was, therefore, understandable that he did not know where the town post office was located. He wanted to mail some letters and decided to go himself, so he asked for directions from a boy of about ten years of age.

"Padre, you take the road going to the market and cut across the stalls (*puesto*). At the other side is a small street. If you turn right and walk straight ahead, you will hit directly on (*tu-tumbukin*) the post office building. It is a one-story structure whose windows have vertical iron bars. You can buy the stamps and leave the letter with the postman. However, Padre, be sure that you cross the new stamps with a ballpen after sticking them on your envelope. That way, your *selyo* (stamps) will not be stolen."

The priest appreciated the detailed directions and the tip on how not to lose stamps and letters. "Thank you very much. You are a kind and helpful boy. You are my first friend here. Please visit me in the *Konvento* (convent) where I stay."

They parted, apparently happy over a promising warm friendship.

The following Sunday, the priest held mass and delivered his inaugural sermon. He was evidently prepared and gave his message with deep feeling. The majority of the parishioners were appreciative and impressed. It was also relevant as he connected his sermon to the current problems of the town and barrios.

However, as he was speaking, his first friend, the ten-year-old boy, sneaked out of the church. Some of the adults also left to smoke outside, returning as soon as the sermon was finished. This was why a loudspeaker was perched on the facade of the church so the smokers could not miss the sermon. The young boy, however, did not return, so he missed the greater part of the sermon.

A few days later, the priest and the young boy met again near the plaza.

"Did you attend school?" asked the priest casually.

"Yes, Padre," the boy answered, averting his eyes.

The priest went directly to the point as they were both in the direct glare of the noontime sun. "Last Sunday was my first sermon. I noticed you left church early and I was disappointed."

"Yes, I did leave early," answered the young boy truthfully.

"Also, my subject was very important. The Way to Heaven' (*Ang Landas Tungo sa Langit*)," said the priest pointedly.

"*Iyon nga, Padre, kaya ako lumabas dahil sa paksa ninyo.*

Paano po akong maniniwala na alam ninyo ang landas patungo sa langit eh hindi nga ninyo alam ang landas patungo sa post office? (That is just it, Padre; the reason I left was because of your topic. How can I believe you know the way to heaven when you don't even know the way to the post office?)"

16

THE PARABLE OF THE BAPTISMAL NAME

The farmer was a nominal church-goer by force of circumstance. The barrio had only a small *kapilya* (chapel), better known as a *bisita* (literally, to visit). The villagers were wont to visit the chapel for only a few minutes before proceeding to their farms. A typical visit would last for no more than a minute or two. A moment to kneel, make a few supplications and perhaps recite the Lord's Prayer or a Hail Mary. Hence, a short visit to the church is called *bisita iglesia.*

No mass was held in the kapilya because there was no regular priest. A yearly mass was held only during the fiesta (birthday of the patron saint). Sometimes there would also be a priest during the *semana santa* (Holy Week).

It was the fiesta so the priest came and a group baptism was held. Before the actual ceremony, the sacristan listed the required data and collected the necessary fees. The official Christian name of the baby was entered into the registry.

The farmer had decided on the name of his son—San Jose. The sacristan would not agree so the priest was called.

"No, you can't name your son San Jose. It is sacrilegious to call him a saint before he has done anything to merit it," explained the priest.

"Okay, Padre," the farmer agreed. "Then I would like to call my son Tiago."

The priest objected again. "You have to call him Santiago."

"But I thought it is prohibited to call him a saint!" remarked the farmer. "Once you make up your mind and can apply the rule consistently I will return to have my child baptized," he said, walking away in a huff.

17

THE PARABLE OF THE BISHOP

The farmer had been neglecting his religious obligations. In particular he missed attending Sunday masses, but not for lack of time or distance from the church. In fact, he went to town every Sunday. But instead of proceeding to church, he sneaked to the *topada* (cockfight matches), although he felt guilty afterwards.

Near his farm was a newly laid out golf course. His sense of guilt was assuaged when he observed the Bishop sneaking out to play on Sundays. Shortly before the farmer left for town, the Bishop would already be on the fairways swinging his clubs. He was playing golf instead of going to church.

"If the Bishop can get away with it, so can I," rationalized the farmer. "He goes to the golf course; I go to the *sabungan* (cockpit)."

The charade went on for years.

The farmer then passed away and found himself confronted by St. Peter. "According to our records," intoned the saint, "you have missed mass practically every Sunday."

"That is true," confessed the farmer.

"Very well, do you have any defense?"

"Well, the church is in town and is too far from my barrio."

"Your facts are accurate except that according to the records, you attended the *sabung* in town religiously every Sunday at the precise time the mass was being celebrated in church."

The farmer bowed his head in shame. "That, too, is true, St. Peter."

"Now, before I send you below, do you have anything else to add?"

The farmer suddenly remembered the Bishop and his Sunday

golf ritual. "I know I am at fault, but, you see, the Bishop in the town did the same. Every Sunday, I saw him sneak to the golf course and play instead of going to church."

"I see," commented St. Peter. "I will do something to punish him."

That Sunday, as usual, the Bishop swung his clubs alone on the fairways. Hole number four was the most difficult and tricky. Not only was there a bend midway in the course but also a sand trap and an artificial lake before the green. It was also the farthest hole covering all of 500 meters.

The Bishop positioned himself and made a great shot, propelling the golf ball like a cannon. As though led by an unseen force, it flew straight to the green and sank into hole number four. It was a hole-in-one!

But no one was around to witness it.

18

THE PARABLE OF THE SEVEN SACKS OF RICE

The farmer was not only hardworking; he was also frugal. At every opportunity he saved what he could by the judicious use of his scarce resources and harvest. While others depleted their supply, he kept his. So a time came when he had saved seven cavans of rice. He knew that someday they would come in handy with the regular coming of calamities.

Soon a strong typhoon came upon the barrio. The winds were accompanied by incessant rains, and then a flood submerged all the ricefields. For five days the water accumulated and rose until it was waist deep. The ripened rice crops just about to be harvested in a few weeks were under water.

Unfortunately, the barrio was like a basin and there was no exit for the water. The grains remained submerged for the duration of the flood and germinated. That year, the rice crop of the whole village was lost.

Hunger haunted the families. Fortunately, the frugal man had his seven cavans of rice. He took pity on his neighbors and, because of his innate generosity, he gave six cavans to his barrio-mates, leaving only one cavan for his own family.

But the neighbors' greed got the better of them and they coveted the seventh sack of rice. So while the frugal man slept in the night, the neighbors stole his remaining cavan of rice.

It is said that man acts in the same way. God in His infinite kindness gave us six days for work, and yet man steals the seventh day which is for rest and worship.

19

THE PARABLE OF THE FOURTH KING

The whole world knows of the three kings—the wise men who travelled far to pay homage to the Baby born in a stable, and to offer Him their gifts of gold, incense and myrrh. They followed the star of Bethlehem in their quest for Baby Jesus.

A little known fact was the fourth king. He, too, was a wise man who journeyed from the east guided by the same star, and who brought his own gift securely fastened to his faithful camel.

But the fourth king did not succeed in his quest. Or so he thought at first. For along the way, he kept making stops. Every time he saw a man in need, he would alight and provide succor.

He overtook a farmer carrying a heavy load. He stopped and offered his camel as he himself alighted and walked.

Near a gully, he found a farmer wounded from the attack of a wild animal. The fourth king tarried for days taking care of the farmer's needs. He refused to continue his journey until the man was brought home to his village.

A group of bandits was pillaging the produce of another farmer. The fourth king again stopped to defend the helpless man.

In the end, the bandits took away his camel and his gift.

So he continued his travel on foot, still stopping and tarrying at every town, where need beckoned him.

Many years passed before the fourth king reached Bethlehem. He was told that the Messiah had proceeded to Jerusalem on a donkey. He rushed over and found a throng of people. They were talking about a Jew who had carried a cross to Calvary.

The fourth king ran and from a distance saw the silhouette of two crosses. A third one was just being erected. At the foot of the Christ nailed on the cross, the fourth king knelt and wept. "I am despicable for tarrying on my journey. I lost my gift, and failed in my quest," he sobbed bitterly.

The Man on the cross spoke in a whisper in a most kindly voice, "Stand. I received your gift long ago and yours is the greatest of them. You found me!"

20

THE PARABLE OF THE RESCUERS

The Governor swam in the lake with his family and a few personal friends. On vacation in the town resort within his area of political coverage, he was in good spirits and felt relaxed in the invigorating waters.

Unfortunately, he was a most unpopular head of the province for he attended more to the accumulation of his personal gains than to the welfare of the people. He was inaccessible and uncaring, not making any attempt to understand the prevailing problems, let alone trying to do something about them. His police force was abusive and his staff was discourteous.

As a whole, the people looked forward to the next elections to unseat this hated head. But that opportunity was two years away. Many people discussed other options to change the unloved Governor, or even get rid of him. All the alternatives were against the law. The only legal one was too far off in the future, and accidents did not just happen. So the Governor remained in power to the great chagrin and frustration of the people.

Meanwhile, the Governor enjoyed his swim in the fresh-water lake. With the feeling of renewal, he became more adventurous and swam towards the deepest part at the center of the lake.

Suddenly, he felt a stiffening of his right leg, and a severe pain shot through all his calf muscles. It was full-blown leg cramps! He flailed his arms and shouted for help. But his family and few friends were poor swimmers, nor were they familiar with the skills of rescuing a drowning person.

By a stroke of good luck, three teenagers passed by. The family of the Governor pleaded for assistance. The three young boys reluctantly undressed and quickly swam towards the center of the lake. The Governor was bobbing in and out. He had swallowed a lot of water.

Soon the three teenagers reached the Governor and propped him up to a prone position. Exhausted and greatly spent, the Governor was dragged with little resistance. A boy pulled him by the hair while the other two held on to an arm each.

On the lake shore, the Governor was placed face down on a long towel. The waist part was maneuvered up to allow water to flow out of his mouth. In a moment, he coughed and the danger to his life was over.

Naturally, the Governor and his family were most thankful. The three boys were instructed to visit the Provincial Capitol for their much-deserved reward.

"You three will be generously compensated for your heroic act of saving my life," proclaimed the Governor. "I will grant anything you wish." He was effusive and in a generous mood. It was a second lease on life for him.

With some difficulty and great reluctance, the three boys expressed their individual great desires.

" I want a job for my father and two older brothers," said the first teenager.

"Go home and tell your father and brothers to report for work tomorrow," announced the Governor.

"I want a concrete house for our family," requested the second boy.

"Go home and consult your parents. Come back tomorrow and tell me where you want the house and the same will be constructed immediately."

The third boy then spoke up, "I want a life-size monument of

34

myself erected at the entrance of the barrio."

The Governor was taken aback by the unusual request. "My boy, that is an easy request to fulfill. Even simpler than jobs and house construction. But, you see, a monument is only erected for dead people."

The third teenager replied, "I understand that, Mr. Governor. But, you see, when the barrio people find out I rescued you, they will surely kill me."

21

THE PARABLE OF THE CARABAO

A farmer and his young son were walking home from the farm along with their carabao.

In a typical barrio houses line both sides of the long main road, and farms are several kilometers away.

By the time the father and the son entered the barrio proper, the young son felt tired. So the father encouraged the son to ride astride the carabao while he continued to walk.

A group noticed the pair and said, "Look at that boy riding on the carabao. What an ill-mannered son! He has no respect for his old father who should be riding instead."

On hearing the comments, the son dutifully alighted and convinced his father to ride on the animal as they proceeded home.

Farther out, another group saw them and commented, "Look at that old man (*matandang kuluban*) riding the carabao. He has no consideration for the young one (*batang musmos*) who should be riding the carabao."

Upon hearing this comment of the barrio people, father and son decided they should both ride on the carabao. And on they went.

Other farmers soon saw them and said within their hearing: "Look at that oppressive farmer and son punishing the carabao. The animal performed its difficult task of plowing the fields the whole day and now these heartless human beings have to ride on its back. How unkind of them!"

Upon hearing these remarks, both father and son got down from the back of the carabao. The three of them—the father, the son and the carabao—all continued walking home.

As they neared their nipa hut, still another group of neighbors saw them and said, "Look at that pair of stupid (*tanga*) father and son. They have a carabao to ride on, yet they are both walking (*may kalabaw ayaw sakyan*)!"

Indeed, there is no perfect action. Anything we do is subject to criticism. Someone will always have some adverse remark about anything one does.

Talk is cheap—that is why there will always be plenty of it around. But when one comes to think of it, what matters most is knowing where one is going. In the final analysis, what others say does not matter. Going to the right place is what counts.

Unfortunately, for the farmer and his son, there was a displacement of goals. They forgot that their original aim was to go home from their farm. Instead they began trying to earn the plaudits of the bystanders.

Detractors in this world are many, but they are better ignored than paid attention to.

22

THE PARABLE OF THE SWINDLER

The man was a born swindler. He gloried in it and spent most of his working hours figuring out how to put one over his tenants. He was very happy knowing that he always got the better part of any arrangement (*nakalamang*). He was the symbol of the robber baron—"a pure predator, completely unscrupulous and unrestrained in his greed."

He was in this mood when he visited one of his tenants to

discuss the system of dividing the harvest from his land. They were sitting on the porch and he addressed the tenant in a solemn tone.

"For this year, let us change our sharing system. No more percentage allocation. We will simplify. Anything above the ground will be mine and all that is below will be yours. Is that acceptable?"

The tenant had no choice. Refusal meant being driven out of the land. There were many who wanted to take over the piece he worked on. "As you wish," the farmer replied with evident reluctance and resignation.

Forthwith the farmer planted peanuts. When harvest time came, he got all the produce from below the ground and the landlord got nothing from his share above the ground.

The man was inwardly furious, but he had to abide by the agreement. However, he was still bent on getting the better part of the deal, so he reversed the agreement for the second year.

"This time you get all the produce above the ground. All the harvest below the ground will be my share," he dictated to the tenant. "Is that agreeable?"

"Yes, whatever you say," replied the farmer with pretended sadness in his voice.

That year, the farmer planted watermelon. He collected all the produce on top of the ground where the vines crawled and gleefully left the roots for his master.

The landlord was very angry and became even more determined to get even. He shouted, "This year, I get all the rootcrops from under the ground. I also get all the produce on the ground and all the harvest from the top of any crop you plant!"

"Then what do I get?" asked the farmer in a contrite tone.

"Well, you get the produce in between, but nothing touching the soil and nothing on top of the plant. Do you understand?" the landlord said with rage and annoyance.

This time the farmer planted corn.

Because the ears were in between the stalks, he got all the produce. No ears of corn touched the ground, none were on top of the stalk, and the roots bore no fruits.

THE PARABLE OF THE FUTURE FATHER-IN-LAW

He was a diligent farmer and a caring father of an only daughter. If arrangements could be agreed upon, he hoped to have a son-in-law soon.

He had reason to be anxious. His daughter was already nineteen years old and by barrio standards, she would be an old maid beyond the age of twenty. Also, her value in the matrimonial market would go down.

For another, the barrio was a small one and there were few desirable young swains. Most of them left the barrio for the city and in many cases they married and settled in the urban centers.

The father's requirements were not too strict, but he wanted a young man dedicated to farming. He wanted someone who could take over his farm when he went to his just reward.

For a full year, the young man had been visiting his daughter. They seemed compatible. So all that was necessary was the formal asking of permission to have his daughter's hand in marriage by the man's parents.

Finally, the father thought the day had come, for the young man formally requested to see the father and not the daughter on that particular Sunday afternoon.

The father was all excited thinking his dream was about to come true. He would soon have his daughter married off to a prospective son-in-law who would take over his farm.

The man arrived at the designated time, all dressed up and his hair gleaming with pomade. Why, he even had on rubber shoes when previously he visited his daughter in his slippers.

"Well, young man, what is it with you? What did you come to see me about?" the older man asked.

"Sir, I have something to ask you," the young man replied with an air of reluctance and hesitation.

"No problem," the prospective father-in-law remarked with enthusiasm and expectation. "I have been waiting for this moment!"

The man became pale and nervous and said, "Sir, you see, I've been wanting to ask you . . ."

"Think nothing of it," interrupted the farmer. "Everything will be arranged. You have my permission to marry my daughter. Here's to your health and future happiness." He poured *tuba* (fermented coconut wine) into two glasses and offered one to his visitor.

"But, sir, I have come to ask you if you would lend me some money," blurted out the young man.

"*Aba, utang pala* (Oh, it's about a loan)!" the old man was taken aback. He continued, "*Hindi pwede kitang pautangin. Eh, ni halos hindi kita kilala* (I can't loan you money. You see, I hardly know you)!"

24

THE PARABLE OF THE LAZY FARMER

The farmer lolled lazily under the mango tree by the roadside. He lay on the incline using the protruding root as his pillow. His *buri* hat was pulled down to cover his eyes and the upper part of his face. A grass reed dangled from his mouth, contentment spread all over his face.

Suddenly, a çar stopped, driving as close to the farmer as the roadside would allow. A man, apparently from the city, wanted to ask some questions.

The farmer removed his hat as a reflex act of courtesy. He sat up and straightened his body.

"We are lost. Can you tell me how far the next town is?" the man asked.

"I don't know," answered the farmer drowsily.

"Does this road lead to San Jose?"

"I don't know."

"Where is the nearest gasoline station?"

"I don't know."

The man was visibly irritated by the farmer's consistent lack of useful information. "What is the matter with you? You don't know anything. You are stupid!" he said in an insulting and overbearing manner.

The farmer looked at him without anger and replied, "I may be stupid, but I am not lost."

The farmer continued to laze free from care and worry under the mango tree.

An elderly official of the town saw and berated the farmer for his seeming laziness and lack of motivation for improvement. "Why don't you work?" he asked in a fatherly tone.

"But what for, *Konsehal* (Councilor)?" the farmer replied.

"So you can have income."

"What will I do with income?"

"Well, you can save it."

"What will I do with savings?"

"You can go on a vacation."

"But what will I do on a vacation?"

The Konsehal thought for a moment and replied, "You can rest and enjoy the scenery."

The farmer brightened up and remarked, "But that is exactly what I am doing now, Konsehal."

25

THE PARABLE OF THE BARRIO GOSSIP

She was the worst gossip in the whole barrio where more than half of the quarrels were due to her incessant rumor-mongering. She was ecstatic when she was able to instigate clashes among the barrio inhabitants.

One day, the woman became very ill. No medicine seemed to help. The illness became intractable and would not respond to any treatment. In desperation, she consulted the barrio *albularyo* (herbalist). His diagnosis was simple and direct to the point. "Your illness is a punishment from God for your excessive penchant for gossiping."

"What should I do to get well?" she asked. "I am willing to do anything to make amends."

"First of all, be sincerely sorry for all the gossiping you've done in your lifetime," admonished the albularyo. "Pray for nine days. When you get well and are strong enough to walk around, get a sack of chicken feathers. Then go to each home and leave one feather in front of their stairs. When you have completed this task, come back to me."

The woman thanked him profusely and made a strong resolve to follow every word of his advice.

As if by a miracle, she got well on the ninth day. Thereupon she got a sack of feathers and visited every house in the barrio. At the foot of each stairs, she left one feather. Upon completion of the requirement, she dutifully reported to the albularyo.

"That is good," commented the albularyo. "Now, return to every house and retrieve each of the feathers you left on the stairs."

She hurriedly visited each of the houses, but, alas, the feathers were gone. All of them had been blown away by the slightest breeze. Sadly, she went back to the albularyo to report her failure to retrieve the feathers.

The wise albularyo had a final word. "You see, gossip is similar to the feathers. Once you utter a false rumor, you cannot take it back. It is blown away, never to be retrieved."

26

THE PARABLE OF THE WINE

The town was in a basically coconut-growing area. As in many places with the same cropping pattern, the people were famous for their superior wine called *lambanog*. Each clan had the capability and inclination to prepare its own produce.

Lambanog is quite a strong drink distilled from the fermentation of coconut sap. In its superior form, the wine is practically all alcohol and resembles ordinary water. In fact, people take pride in igniting their lambanog to demonstrate its high quality.

The people enjoy drinking their lambanog at any time of the day and for any excuse. The favorite occasion, of course, is the town fiesta. Since drinking is usually done in company, a tradition grew in which drinking was held on the Sunday afternoon of the last day of the three-day celebration. The practice involved all men drinking lambanog together in the town plaza.

To increase the fun, each farmer was required to bring his best bottle of lambanog. Each one's contribution was then poured into a huge cauldron which became the common source of drink for everyone. This also became a symbol of their solidarity in a long history of community life related to the coconut industry.

One farmer prepared the bottle for his contribution. But he was not in a sharing mood, so instead of filling the bottle with lambanog, he decided to fill it with ordinary water. He reasoned out that with hundreds of bottles of lambanog, one bottle of water would not be noticed, especially since even on ocular examination one cannot distinguish between lambanog and ordinary water. The only way to tell the difference is by tasting or smelling. But these are not requirements before pouring one's share into the cauldron.

So the farmer brought his water and poured the contents into the cauldron with the rest of the contributed lambanog.

Unfortunately, all the other farmers had the same idea. They also brought along water thinking it would make no difference and no one would notice.

When the celebration began, they partook of the water and parted, all ashamed of themselves.

27

THE PARABLE OF THE SUICIDE

The farmer was despondent. He wanted to end it all, for to him life was no longer worth living.

His wife had deserted him and had run away with another

man. All his grown-up children had left for the city and no one as much as remembered him. A big typhoon followed by a flood ruined his entire rice crop and the winds wrecked his house beyond repair. In the night, robbers stole his furniture and valuables. He was friendless and alone.

He had made up his mind to commit suicide, but the only question was how he would do it.

A knife was too gruesome. He did not have the guts to plunge the kitchen knife into his heart. "Do you do it with one hand or with both hands?" he wondered.

Poison or acid was too messy. The liquid had to pass his mouth and the scorching effect on his throat and esophagus would be unbearable.

Maybe hanging? He would put a rope around his neck and anchor the other end to the rafter on the ceiling, stand on a bucket and kick it from under him. But he heard somewhere that unless the neck bones break, one does not die immediately. Then he would gasp and suffer!

The river was nearby. "But how does one drown himself when he knows how to swim?" he asked himself.

"I will jump from the top of the hill," he thought. But the hill at the edge of the barrio was not steep, and the slopes were grassy. How could one die on such a soft, cushiony surface?

Finally, he remembered the railroad tracks that ran on the other side of the village leading to town. He knew the train rushed by with a loud roar, so he would lie across the tracks. One heavy crack of the iron engine and he'd be dead, gone in a wink. It would all be over with—no pain or awareness.

That was it. So off he went to the railroad tracks and positioned himself firmly across. He waited and waited. And waited.

After two weeks, he died of dehydration from the broiling heat of the sun. And of starvation, too.

The train was late, as usual.

THE PARABLE OF THE WOODEN BOWL

He was basically a good man and an excellent farmer. His harvest was enough for his family to live on comfortably.

There was no reason to complain; the only problem, however, involved his aging mother. Since he had a bigger house, his brothers and sisters placed the old woman under his care.

Feeding her was no problem, but her mind had begun to deteriorate with time. She was still aware of people, although more and more she would stare blankly at nothing in particular.

She ate well and was not choosy about food. The only aberration was her tendency to drop her plate on the floor. Whenever a plate crashed anywhere, they knew she was the cause. So it was decided that she be made to eat from a wooden bowl. She could then drop the bowl without causing any loss.

The farmer had an eight-year-old son who loved to tinker and do small carpentry work. He produced crude toys by nailing together discarded pieces of wood. Occasionally, he would get empty tin cans and convert them into creative and unique toy vehicles. His favorite material for wheels consisted of four soda pop caps (*tansan*).

One day, instead of toys, the boy began to chisel on a piece of wood. No one could tell what it was. After a few days, they still could not guess what he was making. Up to that point, the figure had been roundish.

The father asked his young son, "What are you doing?"

The boy looked up and announced proudly, "I am making a wooden bowl for you to eat from when you grow old, Papa."

THE PARABLE OF THE MYSTERIOUS LAKE

In a distant town, a long time ago, there was a mysterious lake. It teemed with various fishes but they had the uncanny habit of remaining at the bottom. Since the lake was many fathoms deep, the people could not take advantage of this natural resource.

Meanwhile, in spite of the teeming lake, the people were hungry. They had a shortage of grains and very little animal supplements.

It was in the midst of this irony that a farmer among them revealed a supernatural ability. He claimed he had the prowess to siphon off huge quantities of water in his mouth. So the people requested him to take out the water in the lake so that all of them could gather the fish at the bottom.

At first, the farmer was reluctant for it was a delicate process. But seeing the hunger and malnutrition all around, he finally relented.

However, he had one specific condition. "I will siphon off all the water from the lake and retain it in my mouth. However, I can only hold my breath for exactly three minutes. Within that period you must gather all the fish you can get. When the time is up I will wave my hands. You must all get out of the lake for I will then let go the water from my mouth, and the lake will return to its original depth."

"But why only three minutes?" the people complained. "We need more time to catch the fish."

"Three minutes because that is all the time I can retain the huge volume of water in my mouth," the farmer replied. "And, also, the amount of fish you can gather in that time is all you need to be well fed for a whole week."

They all agreed to have the lake dried up the next day. All the townspeople appeared, for the good news had spread all over town. Even children came with their parents. They surrounded the big lake, and there was almost no space open at the edge of the water line.

At the appointed time, the farmer reminded them of the three-minute limit. With hushed expectation, the people saw the farmer dip his lips in the water. Slowly at first, then with a tremendous suction, the lake began to recede. The fish appeared and the lake was soon a dry bed.

The people rushed in and began picking up all the fish within sight. All were able to get at least a dozen each.

After exactly three minutes, the farmer waved both hands as his signal. Everyone scampered out with their catch still struggling. Many had brought baskets, and others even put the fish in their pockets, shouting with joy at the bounty of their harvest.

In a wink, water gushed from the farmer's mouth. It took only a minute for the lake to return to its former appearance and depth.

The next week, the same procedure and excitement were repeated. This time more came, for people from nearby towns had heard about the blessings from the man who siphoned off the water. All went well and the people got plenty of fish within three minutes.

On the third week, still more came. People from the adjoining provinces had heard the good news and wanted to have a share of the harvest.

As in the past two sessions, the farmer warned all about the three-minute limit and his hand signals for clearing the bed. He then sipped all the water.

The supply of fish seemed inexhaustible. People filled baskets, cans and even sacks with fish.

At the precise moment, the farmer waved his hands. But the people continued to gather the jumping fish, disregarding the frantic waving of the farmer.

He could no longer hold the water in his mouth. In a burst of fury the water spurted out. The lake immediately filled up, drowning all the people in it.

Hunger did not kill them. Greed did.

THE PARABLE OF THE DYING HUSBAND

The farmer lay on his deathbed. He felt his strength ebbing, so he closed his eyes trying to build up enough energy for his parting words.

His wife hovered around, attending to his needs. She was resigned and ready for the worst.

The sick man beckoned to his wife, so she dutifully approached him. As his voice was very faint, she bent over to catch every word. It was a confession of past misdeeds.

"I am about to go to that place beyond (*kabilang buhay*)," he began with great effort. "Before I finally leave, I want to make a clean breast of all my misdeeds."

"There is no need," she replied. "Just calm down your feelings (*ipanatag ang kalooban*) and rest. God will take care of your past transgressions. Bury your sins with yourself."

"No, I insist," he replied, breathing hard. "I feel that I must unburden myself. The load is too heavy to carry any farther."

The wife looked at him with an emotionless face. "Go ahead if it will make you feel better, and you feel you're strong enough to talk."

"You see," he whispered, "our carabao that got lost did not really disappear. Instead, I sold it in the next town. I squandered all the money gambling in the *sabungan* (cockpit)."

She remained calm and expressionless. "I know, and I understand."

"Furthermore," he continued, "remember the sale of our pineapples? I told you I lost the money to pickpockets in the market. That wasn't really true. I spent the money on drinking and nightclubbing."

His wife continued looking at him without anger. There was no hint of judgment in her voice as she replied, "I know. And I understand."

"And, finally," his voice almost trailed to a stop, "I mortgaged our land and never repaid the loan. So we no longer own the farm. I used the money to maintain another woman in town."

Still the wife's composure held. "Don't worry. I know and I understand," she said in a hushed voice.

"You are a great woman," he sighed with tears in his eyes. "I do not deserve you. So is everything now all right?"

For the first time, her face hardened. With a sneer she told him, "Yes, everything is now all right. You see, I was the one who poisoned you."

31

THE PARABLE OF THE BROTHERS

A farmer had a young brother. They grew up together sharing everything that came their way.

As time went by, the older brother got married, and with the wife's help their farm progressed and their wealth increased. They filled their home with every conceivable amenity—a television set, a stereo hi-fi, a sala set, a gas refrigerator and even a tricycle. The last was hired out whenever the family had no need for mobility.

Meanwhile, the younger brother somehow remained destitute. His crops did not do well. The yield was low and barely enough to sustain his own needs. He naturally approached his older brother for help.

By then, the older brother had a circle of friends around him. They came to drink his wine and to tell him what a great guy he was. Late every afternoon they came and left shortly before midnight. He was generous with his food and joined them in watching his TV set.

When the younger brother came, the older brother would not see him. On several more occasions, he was too busy with his bootlicking friends and freeloaders. The younger brother could only see his brother's wife—but even she could not persuade her husband to see and help his brother.

She then decided to do something about the anomalous situation. To start with, she was fed up with the nightly crowd. She had to attend to their needs, leaving her sleepless and tired. More and more, the unwelcome visitors demanded attention. They had become a nuisance.

On the other hand, she felt the younger brother needed a break. For, in earlier times, the young man had helped the older brother sharing with him what little harvest he had, even denying himself fruits and vegetables so his older brother's family could have more.

One day, the older brother's wife killed a dog, wrapped it in a buri mat and placed the bundle in a corner of the yard. She then told her husband of a fatal tragedy. She narrated how she discovered a dirty-looking boy stealing from their rice bin (*kamalig*). She said she hit him with a bamboo pole with no intention of hurting him but only to scare him away. The boy leaped out of the kamalig and hit his head on a rock. Now the boy was bloody and lifeless, wrapped in a mat.

"Let us ask your friends to help bury the body," she pleaded.

"Yes, my friends will all come to help," the husband said with confidence.

But no one came to help. The so-called friends and drinking partners refused to be involved. Why, they might even be named accessories to the crime!

The older brother was disappointed and frantic. "What should we do?" he asked his wife. "I need help to bury the body in the forest."

"Let us ask your brother," she suggested, perking up with assured assistance.

Reluctantly, the older brother agreed. "Let us call him," he sighed with a heavy heart. He knew he had been mean and neglectful, even selfish and heartless.

Immediately, the younger brother arrived. Without any hesitation, he helped carry the wrapped body to the deep forest. Together they buried the evidence of the crime at night under the cover of darkness.

The next day the police arrived. The older brother's friends had reported him to the authorities. "We saw the dead boy dripping with blood," they chorused. "Look in that corner of the yard and you will see traces of the dastardly act."

True enough, small pools of dried blood were visible. Even the wooden fence was splattered with blood stains. There was no denying it.

"Where is the body?" asked the policeman with a stern voice. "You have killed a boy. These civic-minded men reported the crime. Now I see it is true. The blood is all over the place. You had better

49

confess and tell us where you have disposed of the evidence."

Reluctantly, the older brother and his wife led them to the site. The barrio people followed as the news about the murder quickly spread. A big crowd witnessed the actual exhumation of the body.

After some digging, the buri mat wrapping appeared. The people gasped in horror. The police looked at the couple with a sneer reserved for criminals. The older brother bowed his head in shame. His wife kept quiet beside him. The younger brother was on the other side bravely facing the crowd, ready for the worst.

When the buri mat was unfolded, they all saw a dead dog!

Now, the older brother realized who his real friend was. He asked his younger brother to stay with them and took care of his needs.

The wife was happy for the nightly disturbance stopped.

The younger brother was happy. They were brothers again, thanks to the cunning scheme of the older brother's wife.

32

THE PARABLE OF THE STINGY SONS

A farmer worked himself to the bone for he was driven by an obsessive dream. He wanted his two sons to get an education because he himself had failed to get one because of poverty. He had only reached the fifth grade in the barrio school. He had started to farm even while still a teenager.

Normally, the son of a farmer would also be a farmer all his life; so would his children; and his children's children. He did not want this fate for his two sons. He wanted his children to have everything he had never had in material comforts and educational attainment.

His efforts were rewarded. In time one son became a lawyer and the other finished an accounting course. The two sons moved permanently to the city to practice their respective professions. They did well and became wealthy and raised their families.

As time passed, however, they conveniently neglected and sometimes actually forgot their father.

"*Nakalimutan na ang pinanggalingan* (They have forgotten where they came from)," the father would mutter. This is really the first line of a popular local proverb, which continues: "*Ay hindi makararating sa paroroonan* (cannot reach his destination)."

His invitations to his sons were always turned down for reasons of time constraints. The two sons never as much as sent him even a measly peso.

Finally, the father convinced the sons to visit by inviting the grandchildren to the barrio fiesta, so they could see their roots.

The lawyer arrived first. After the amenities, the son gave the father a picture. "You see, father, it is so cumbersome to bring the pig from the city to the barrio. It would also dirty our car. So I brought you the picture of the pig."

"Thank you," the father acknowledged without revealing his feelings.

Then the second son arrived. An accountant, he was now a man of means. He also produced a picture and handed it to his father. "This is the picture of a house that I want to build for you in the city. But I know you prefer to live in the barrio, so I have brought you a picture instead."

"Many thanks," the father said simply.

At noon, the two sons and their families were hungry. As tradition would have it, they expected a sumptuous lunch with at least six courses.

"When do we eat, Father?" they asked.

"Please proceed to the dining table. Everything is ready there now," the father announced.

They all eagerly proceeded to the inner room beside the old kitchen. The table was bare, except that on top were cut-outs from magazines. All were pictures of sumptuous food including fried chicken, *lechon*, *morkon*, vegetable stew, *pancit* and steaming rice, complete with clippings of fruits, ice cream, macapuno, and *halaya*.

THE PARABLE OF THE DIAGNOSES

Three barrio *albularyos* (herb doctors) once sat together (*naguumpukan*) exchanging experiences, recent cases and sure-fire treatments. Soon their conversation shifted to bragging about their special abilities to diagnose patients. Each claimed the knack for diagnosing anyone's illness just by looking at him. No one wanted to be outdone by the others.

An elderly woman who overheard their claims had an excellent suggestion. "There is a man walking slowly towards us with a peculiar gait, holding his waist. Now you each state your diagnosis. As soon as he reaches us we can verify directly from him what really ails him. Then we will know who has made the best diagnosis among you three."

The albularyos agreed. Intently, they observed the approaching man.

The first albularyo decided fast. "I know what ails him. He has a stomachache. Look at the way he holds his waist."

The second albularyo announced his diagnosis. "No, not stomachache. I am sure he has a backache, because look at his hunched appearance. His back is troubling him."

The third was also ready with his pronouncement. "You're both wrong. The man is suffering from rheumatism of the right knee. Notice how he limps? He is using his left leg to support his body. The right knee pains him."

Soon the man was just across from them. The elderly woman asked him, "*Ano ho ba ang nararamdaman ninyo? May sakit ba kayo?* (What do you feel? Are you sick?)"

The man looked surprised. He stopped and straightened himself. "*Wala ho akong nararamdaman. At lalo namang wala akong sakit. Papunta lang ako sa palikuran para dumumi.* (I don't feel anything. Moreover, I have no ailment. I'm just on my way to the toilet to relieve myself.)"

All three could not help laughing at their wrong presumptions.

Meanwhile, the elderly woman admonished them: "*Kaya kayo, sa uli-uli ay huwag gamot ng gamot. Tanungin muna ang dinaramdan ng pasyente para malaman ang sakit. Ganoon din sa nayon. Huwag paun-lad ng paunlad ng proyekto. Tanungin muna ang suliranin at panga-ngailangan ng tao.* (So, next time, don't treat and treat indiscriminately. Ask the patient first what he feels, so you will know the ailment. The same goes for our village. Don't just go on and on with projects. Ask the people first what their problems and needs are.)"

34

THE PARABLE OF THE GODFATHER

The farmer was a well known tightwad. He was extremely frugal, to the point of selfishness. If he could help it, he would refuse to part with a single centavo, and hoarded his money like a miser.

Yet he had social obligations to fulfill. He was godfather to a young boy in the barrio.

The young boy knew his godfather was liberal with excuses but was unwilling to give anything. Even then, the boy decided to pay his respects. After all, he was still his *ninong* (godfather) and he was obligated by custom to kiss his hand on special occasions.

"*Mano po, ninong* (Kiss your hand, godfather)," the boy greeted, clutched the farmer's hand and reverently passed the backside of the palm on his own forehead.

"*Pagpalain at kaawaan ka ng Poong Maykapal* (May the Lord bless and have mercy on you)," the godfather responded with all solemnity.

After the amenities, the boy requested permission to leave. That moment was important for, traditionally, a godfather hands money to a respectful and thoughtful godson.

"Do you have a piggy bank?" asked the godfather.

"No, ninong, I do not have one," replied the boy.

"It's a pity because if you had one, I wanted to drop some coins in it."

The boy left disappointed. But there was always a next time. On the following special occasion, the boy again dutifully visited his godfather. The same amenities transpired and he was ready to depart.

"Do you have a piggy bank?" asked the godfather.

"Yes, yes, ninong, I have one," exclaimed the boy. "In fact, I brought it with me."

"It's a pity because if you had none, I would have given you money to buy one."

35

THE PARABLE OF THE JIGSAW PUZZLE

The farmer was taking his usual noonday siesta on the bare floor of the small living room. His children were out in the yard shouting intermittently. He was interrupted every time a burst of noise pierced through the open window and the spaces of the bamboo slats on the floor.

Three times he asked them to keep quiet. They did for a while, but soon came again the shrill shouts of the children. He decided to do something about it by providing them a substitute diversion.

On a side table was an old magazine. He ripped off a page with a map of the world. Carefully, he tore the sheet into many tiny squares. Then he called his children in and announced: "I have a game for you. It is called jigsaw puzzle. The object of the game is to fit the pieces together until you complete the page showing the map of the world. When you complete the task, let me know as I have a prize for you."

The children got the pieces of the puzzle and scampered to the yard. Quietly and with concentration, they tried to fit each section. In shredded form, the magazine page had over a hundred pieces. That was difficult enough. But to make heads and tails of a map with only lines and black and white colors—that was really tricky and time-consuming.

"Ah, smart me," the father murmured to himself with satisfaction. "Now I can take a really restful and quiet siesta for at least a full hour. Then I will feel fresh and ready for the afternoon work at my farm."

After fifteen minutes, the children were back with the jigsaw puzzle completed. The farmer could not believe it, but there it was—the map of the world in its original form from the old magazine!

"How did you do it?" the farmer asked, unable to get over his amazement.

The oldest child answered, "You know, Father, at the back of the page is the picture of a man. We fitted in parts of the broken man and the world behind him became whole again."

36

THE PARABLE OF THE TIDAL WAVE

In a barrio by the seashore lived a hermit. He chose to build his hut away from the cluster of nipa huts along the beach, all a stone's throw from the water line. The hermit's hut was at the edge of the barrio on top of a hill overlooking the sea.

The majority of the inhabitants earned a living by fishing, so they chose to live close to the water.

The hermit planted upland rice, corn and some vegetables on the hill. He loved the site of his hut and farm for it was isolated by a steep slope from the barrio below. Very few people bothered to climb and that suited the hermit very well, for he truly wanted to be alone.

The fishermen ridiculed the hermit for his odd ways. They made fun of him but they left him to do his own thing.

The view from his hut exhilarated the hermit. On a clear day, he could see the horizon. Sometimes he could see the faint silhouette of large ships sailing by. The silvery water of the sea contrasted with the blue of the sky. Below, he saw the sandy beach studded with the makeshift huts of the fishermen. Bamboo poles on which nylon fishing nets hung to dry in the sun pointed skywards. Tiny boats were anchored parallel to one another, their outriggers spread out. With this view and enough food to eat, the hermit lived in peace and solitude.

One day, as he looked out at the sea, he saw a huge wave. He had watched the horizon often but the waves were never that large. It was like an enormous mattress being rolled towards the barrio below.

"My God," he gasped, "a tidal wave is coming. There must have been an undersea volcanic eruption."

His first concern was the welfare and safety of the fishermen and their families below. He thought of rushing down to alert them. But that would take at least ten minutes even if he ran. By that time the tidal wave would be halfway to the shore. Then the people would need another ten minutes to run up the hill for safety—that is, if he had enough time to go from house to house and the people would take his warning seriously. Chances were, the inhabitants would quickly conclude that the hermit had gone mad.

True enough, as the hermit thought out his next step, the huge waves moved closer. There was very little time to avert a major tragedy. There was only one thing to do.

He started a fire and ignited his hut. Next he set fire to his upland rice whose grains had just started ripening. With the wind the cogon grass around was easily kindled into angry flames. Soon the hill was ablaze with fire and dark smoke.

The inhabitants in the seashore barrio saw the conflagration. They all knew it was the hermit's hut and farm. Following the tradition of neighborly assistance, the people rushed to the slope and climbed it with much effort.

When they reached the top, all that remained were ashes and the smoldering embers of tree branches and bamboo slats. The hut was completely gone and the farm entirely ruined.

The hermit stood looking at the village below. As the people turned their gaze towards the sea, their frightened eyes saw the tidal waves as big as iron ships. The onrushing water engulfed their huts and boats like match- sticks in a turbulent river. It was as though the floodgates of an irrigation dam were suddenly opened, unleashing a cascade of water submerging the whole barrio.

They had lost their homes and fishing nets. But their lives had been saved and their faith in the goodness of humanity restored through the supreme sacrifice of the hermit.

THE PARABLE OF THE DULLEST BOY

He was the son of a farmer. At home and in school, the boy was known for his clumsiness and propensity for doing things wrong.

The barrio teacher gave up on him. He could barely read and could never add the simplest numbers. Even after several years he could not understand what percent meant. He passed the fourth grade after three years, and only out of the teacher's pity. His parents suspected that the teachers wanted to get rid of him. By then they realized that school was not for their son. He was getting too old for his classmates.

"I will teach him to farm," the farmer decided.

But the boy was so slow in comprehension, he could not learn the basics of farm work. The carabao got lost when he grazed the animal. He could not guide the plow in a straight line. The rice seedlings withered because he nipped off the roots. He was assigned to watch the water level and he ended up draining the rice fields of the precious commodity when he opened the irrigation gates.

In exasperation, the father gave up. "Farming is not for him."

"Maybe he is good for nothing," agreed the mother.

Finally, a solution came. An aunt in the city needed a store-helper. The boy was sent. "The city might help him make a little something of himself," sighed the father.

The barrio referred to the boy as bobo or dull, but in school he was known as the *pinakabobo* (dullest). He was picked as the "student least likely to succeed."

After he left, the barrio was only too happy to get rid of him and quickly forgot about this "dullest boy." Even his parents did not bother to check on him for fear he was making a nuisance of himself and might be returned to the village.

Many years passed. One day, the boy came back to the barrio. He was no longer a boy but a young man. He rode a chauffeur-driven Mercedes Benz E600. His face had not changed, although the rough edges of irresponsibility had been softened and toned down. Now he sported a tailored suit and Florsheim shoes. He carried an attache case matching his coat.

His family and the neighbors could not believe their eyes. But there was no mistake—it was certainly he!

He opened his attache case and with flair handed a thick wad of money to his mother. Then he distributed crisp one-hundred-peso bills to every one milling around.

"How did you become so rich? I hope you did not do anything improper or against the law," his mother said, clutching tightly at the unbelievable amount of money. She had never held so much money at any one time in her whole life.

"No, Mother, strictly business and proper," he said.

"Tell us how," his father prodded him.

"Yes, tell us," said the old barrio teacher who came to join the crowd. The news of his return to the village had spread like cogon fire.

"I do buying and selling," he explained. "You know, I buy an item and sell by adding five percent."

"Just like that and you are now a millionaire? Give us the details," chorused the crowd.

"Well, for example, I buy corn at one peso, then I sell at six pesos. You see, just add five percent and the business will surely prosper."

38

THE PARABLE OF THE SMART LAWYER

The company borrowed the farmer's carabao. The animal was to be used as a prop to add authenticity and color to their program. An important visiting dignitary was to be entertained with a lavish indoor barrio fiesta.

Arches and small pennants were strung across the auditorium. A one-sided nipa hut was constructed, complete with roof and a swinging window for the *harana* (serenade) number. A hay loft was put in. A real *lechon* was roasted on a make-believe pile of unlighted charcoal.

The company lawyer had a bright idea. "Let's borrow a

carabao," he suggested, "and leash it near the hay loft to graze. A carabao is a mild animal so it will not cause any problem. It will stay where you tie it. The effect will be realistic and dramatic."

The whole group thought this was an excellent and clever gimmick. So they borrowed the work animal of the farmer nearby.

The party was a huge success. The carabao was the star of the show as it occasionally cowered during the tinikling dance. The clapping of the bamboo poles scared the animal to the great amusement of the crowd. For a finale, the carabao splattered a pile of dung beside the hay loft.

After the program, the animal was brought out and tied loosely to a fence. Unfortunately, the carabao pulled off and soon roamed the familiar grazing fields.

The following day, the carabao was nowhere to be found. Naturally, the farmer claimed his carabao's fair value. A working and well-trained carabao is worth a substantial amount. But the company had no line budget for such an item. They hedged and delayed settlement until a way could be found. The company lawyer was called in. "Don't worry, I will take care of the farmer. I'll confuse him with legalities and bureaucracy until he accepts a smaller sum," the lawyer boasted.

The following day, the lawyer and the farmer met in the small conference room. As agreed, the lawyer's perorations were a jargon beyond the comprehension of the farmer. But he dutifully listened.

"You see, we did not sign a binding Deed of Conveyance. Neither was there an Instrument for Compensation. So, no Agreement. The issue at bar is what, out of benevolence, the company should award you. We are prepared to pay one half the value of your beast of burden upon your signing a Quit Claim."

The farmer agreed meekly, got the money and returned home.

The day before, he had found his carabao grazing contentedly near the familiar bamboo grove.

THE PARABLE OF THE DISTANCE

A farmer sat under a spreading camachile tree by the wayside fanning himself with a *buri* hat. His carabao was wallowing nearby in a small mud puddle. They were waiting for the sun to set a little before continuing to till the land.

A man from town stopped to ask the farmer a question. "Hey, Mr. Farmer, can you tell me how many minutes it will take me to reach the river from where we are now?"

The farmer looked at him but said nothing.

The man repeated the question, thinking the farmer might not have understood. "Mr. Farmer, you see, I want to go to the river on foot. I want to know how long in minutes it will take me."

The farmer remained quiet.

Suspecting the farmer was hard of hearing, the man shouted, "I am asking, how many minutes will it take me from here to the river on foot?"

Still the farmer said not a word.

The man was now sore, and walked towards the river in a huff.

"Twenty minutes," shouted the farmer when the man was about fifteen meters away.

The man looked back and said with evident anger, "I asked you thrice and you refused to tell me. Now that I am on my way, you finally shout it to me. Why didn't you answer while I was near?"

"How could I tell how long it would take you," answered the farmer standing, "since I had not yet seen how fast you walk!"

THE PARABLE OF THE MOON

The tribe lived at the foot of the mountain, isolated from other barrios. The tribesmen foraged in the forest. Wild animals and fruits were available and, occasionally, they slashed and burned. There was food for everyone.

When a wild boar was killed with an arrow, the meat was shared among all the families. Their term for food was the same as that for sharing. Hatred and war were unknown to the people.

For bartering purposes, some men of the village produced crude charcoal. They gathered branches from the trees and burned them in a hole in the ground. When ready, they put out the flames by scooping up loose soil and throwing it into the hole.

One day, a hunter wandered into the hamlet. This was rare for few had reached their isolated mountain place. The villagers were cordial. They offered him water, sweet potatoes and dried meat of wild boar.

The hunter was invited to spend the night in the hamlet. There was a three-quarter moon, and the people stayed in the yard in front of their chief's hut. They talked and chanted tunes, using nose flutes and brass gongs.

The hunter wanted to test the general comprehension and outlook of the people. He asked, "What is better to you, the sun or the moon?"

The tribe spokesman answered, "The moon!"

The hunter was surprised to hear the opposite of what he had expected to hear. So he asked why.

"Because the sun comes out when it is already bright, while the moon comes out to provide light when it is dark."

THE PARABLE OF THE MICE

In Barrio Daga, there was a serious problem. For the past month, a huge cat that lived nearby had been devouring a dozen mice each mealtime. Unless they did something soon, all the mice in the barrio were threatened with complete extinction. In fact, after just a month, barely half of their original number remained.

The best minds in Barrio Daga met to thresh out a solution, but without apparent success. Finally, one suggested they go to the next town and consult a mouse famous for his planning ability.

The leaders wasted no time in visiting this famous planner because every mealtime meant more deaths for the mice of Barrio Daga. It was literally a race against time.

The famous planner listened intently. The problem boiled down to a huge cat that stealthily and regularly descended upon the mouse population at mealtime and feasted on them.

Almost immediately the famous planner had a sure-fire solution, and said without hesitation: "Very simple! All you have to do is make sure you have a way of knowing when the cat is coming so you can all scamper to safety. Your problem springs from the surprise element that spells your death. I have just the right plan. You must provide the cat with a bell on its tail. This way, when the cat approaches, his tail would wag and thus automatically ring the bell tied on the tip of its tail. With that signal, you will all have enough time to run to your safe hiding places out of reach of the cat."

The mice were ecstatic with joy at the wonderful solution. They could not contain their great happiness and thanked the famous planner profusely. They even paid the expert a handsome fee.

So back went the leader mouse to Barrio Daga with the perfect solution to their very serious problem. This was announced and, as expected, everyone was filled with excitement at the impending end to their constant danger.

But one young mouse had a small question. "Excuse me, sirs. I know the solution is terrific and effective. But how do we tie the bell to the cat's tail?"

It was indeed a legitimate point. Unfortunately, no one could provide an adequate and practical answer. So the leaders decided to go back to the famous planner who had given them the brilliant idea of a warning bell.

The oldest of the mice spoke for the group. "Mr. Expert Planner, the whole population of Barrio Daga is indebted to you for your excellent solution to our deadly problem. However, we are at a loss as to how to put the bell on the cat's tail."

The famous planner looked at the delegation impassively as he replied, "Gentlemice, I am a planner. I do not take care of implementation."

42

THE PARABLE OF THE PLOWMAKER

The farmer was also the town's most able and well-known plowmaker. He crafted each piece with care. Other farmers from all over the province came to buy plows and to admire his skill.

He personally shaped the handle. No crevice could be seen, for the surface was scraped clean and polished. The blade was carefully curved to just the right angle. Soil would slide and turn around along the furrows through the gleam of the metal. Every wooden piece came from hardwood aged and well dried.

For years, he made perfect plows and sold many pieces to countless grateful cultivators.

One day, a buyer arrived from out of town. He wanted a larger plow that could be hitched to two carabaos. That way, more land could be worked on. He offered double payment.

The plowmaker complied. He made a medium plow good for two work animals and received double payment.

Sometime later, another buyer from another province arrived. He wanted an even bigger plow—one that could be pulled by three carabaos. And he offered to pay four times the normal cost of a regular plow.

The plowmaker was happy to fill the order. For about the same effort and a little increase in materials, he would increase his income four-fold.

The buyer was greatly satisfied. He made the payment and left.

The plowmaker had an idea. If a big plow accrued him four times more money, why not make only one huge type? It called for the same skill and craftsmanship. "I will become rich," he gleefully said to himself.

From that day on, he only built the biggest plows. He stacked them for the buyers to come. Occasionally, he would figure out the expected four-fold increase in his income.

But no one came. He had overlooked the fact that all the farmers in his town owned only one carabao each.

43

THE PARABLE OF THE OLD PLOW

The farmer brought his old plow (*araro*) to the plowmaker because he wanted to change it for just the right plow. He wanted a blade slanted with just the right curve to turn the soil inside out. The tip should be sharp enough to dig into the driest earth but blunt enough to withstand hitting a hard rock. The frame must be sturdy but should not be so heavy as to strain his muscles unnecessarily. The handle should be just right up to his waistline from a slight bend. The grip must fit his palms comfortably.

The farmer thought his ideas perfect, so he examined each plow carefully. From the blade to the frame to the handle, somehow a feature would invariably not satisfy him. If the bend was right, the handle was not to his liking, and the blade was not curved properly. He admired a plow whose frame was made of pure hard wood—just the right finish for him—but he found it too heavy to balance, let alone to lift. One plow had just the correct bend to the blade but the pointer was too blunt for efficient cutting of the furrow.

Finally, near the entrance to the store was a plow. It had all the features he wanted. The blade was just right with the proper curve and tip. The frame was sturdy and light enough. The length of the handle was right up to his waist. And the grip fitted so well, his thumb and fingers seemed to sink in its proper groove in the handle.

The farmer asked the plowmaker if he could have the plow. It turned out to be his old plow.

44

THE PARABLE OF THE CENTIPEDE

It was the world of animals—a place where the centipede, the rats, the cats and dogs lived and cared for each other. Even the birds and chickens were there. In the active life of animals, the success of one was the success of all. And the problem of each was the concern of everybody.

The movable Mr. Centipede (*alupihan*) had a problem. He felt extremely tired at the end of the day. Where every other species had plenty of energy left, poor Mr. Centipede was exhausted and spent.

"This is not fair," he complained. "Why should I be deprived of further activity when nightfall comes? Why shouldn't I have the same pep as others in the animal kingdom? Maybe something is the matter with me. Yes, maybe I am sick."

His friends advised him to visit Dr. Rooster, the best physician and diagnostician in the whole kingdom. Because he continued to be easily fatigued, Mr. Centipede agreed to consult the doctor.

As expected, Doc Rooster was most sympathetic and thorough in his examination. The doctor looked into every part of Mr. Centipede's body and all his systems. Complete laboratory tests were ordered. Everything turned out negative and unremarkable. So Mr. Centipede was given a clean bill of health and dismissed without medication except some advice to rest each time he got overly fatigued.

Unfortunately, Mr. Centipede did not notice any change in his fatigue pattern. At the end of the day, he was fagged out. This he could not accept as he needed to move around especially at night.

Finally, Mr. Centipede consulted Dr. Owl. Although the consultation fee was much higher, he felt the situation was desperate and called for specialized treatment and advanced consultation.

But the expense was well worth it. One look and Dr. Owl ascertained the problem and immediately prescribed the answer. "Your situation is really simple," he said with complete assurance. "Your problem comes from your hundred legs. You get tired because you use too many extremities. You spend so much energy moving all your legs so that at the end of the day you are fully spent."

This sounded reasonable although Mr. Centipede had never thought of his legs as the problem. He wanted a solution. "Dr. Owl, I'm so relieved to know the cause of my fatigue. Please give me the solution."

Without even thinking, Dr. Owl had the answer. "Because your problem is in your extremely numerous legs, the solution is to reduce them to four. Look at the active rat. He can scamper around the whole day and still have enough energy to run around at night. He manages because of only four legs while you have a hundred of them. So reduce your legs to four like the rat and other more sensible animals."

"Thank you so much, Dr. Owl," effused Mr. Centipede with deep feeling. "Now, how do I accomplish that?"

Dr. Owl answered with annoyance and evident impatience, "Mr. Centipede, please do not bother me with details."

45

THE PARABLE OF THE NEW HAMPSHIRE COCKEREL

The barrio subsisted on the poultry industry. In fact, the town was called the egg basket of the region. Egg production was substantial and even the broilers for chicken meat netted the farmers a comfortable income.

But as time passed, the egg-laying capacity of the hens subsided. Even the meat of the culled chickens was lighter. Added to these were the increasingly prohibitive cost of feeds and the competition of the huge commercial poultry outfits.

Many farmers stopped or reduced their poultry involvement. The chickens decided to meet and do something to save their impending annihilation almost by default.

"What is happening to us?" asked the elderly rooster. "I can't believe the egg-laying capability of our wives has gone this low. Even our meat is decreasing."

"Maybe after all these years we are getting tired," piped in a young hen.

They exchanged ideas—some foolish, others more practical. A wise rooster shared the information that in the next village, they had invited a New Hampshire cockerel to upgrade the flock. As a result, the egg-laying capacity of the succeeding generation doubled. Even the meat was likewise doubled.

The native roosters, faced with no alternative, reluctantly decided to invite a New Hampshire cockerel to their village. Fortunately, only one was needed and this mitigated the feelings of the local breed.

Everyone waited for the results with bated breath. The New Hampshire cockerel wandered around freely. He was seen talking to the hens and seemed available at any time of the day. The food and way of life suited him and no complaint was heard. After all, he received special treatment even if this was expensive to maintain in a poor village.

After a full year, the chicken population decided to meet again to assess the results of the great experiment in upgrading.

The native roosters were particularly eager to know the results. After all, the presence of the imported rooster had caused a lot of uncertainty and inferiority complex among the younger ones.

A close look at the statistics was most revealing. There was neither increase in egg-laying rate nor in chicken meat. After all the expense, special privileges and ill- feelings, the results were certainly not acceptable. There was a lot of howling and condemnation. But the level-headed chickens had a point: "Let us find out and at least ask Mr. New Hampshire cockerel." So they did.

"How come no improvement has occurred after your one-year stay here?" asked the head rooster.

"Oh," exclaimed the New Hampshire cockerel, "I am a consultant and only give advice. I do not implement."

46

THE PARABLE OF THE SINGING BIRD

The egg had just hatched, producing the little featherless bird (*inakay*). The nest was nice and cozy. However, a sudden gust of strong wind dislodged the nest from the branch of a tree and down fell the poor little bird on the open ground below.

Without feathers for protection, the bird began to turn bluish as it shivered in the morning breeze. In a few hours, the little bird would perish from the harsh elements.

By a stroke of good luck, a young boy on his way to school saw the shivering bird and took pity on it. He picked it up, cradled it in his cupped hand, and gently blew some warm air on it. The boy would have loved to keep the bird for a pet but he knew the poor featherless thing was too weak to survive.

He looked around for a suitable nesting place but couldn't find any. All he saw was a fresh mound of carabao dung on the ground. The boy tenderly placed the bird in the middle of the mound and buried the whole body, with only the head and part of the neck protruding. The mound was still warm so the bird felt good. Its blood began to circulate. In half an hour the bird felt so comfortable that it began to sing.

A farmer on his way to his ricefield heard the singing and saw the bird buried in the mound of dung. He thought the poor thing was in distress so he bent down and pulled it out. The farmer even wiped away the adhering excrement and then laid the bird on the grassy part of the roadside.

Soon the sun began to warm the bird. The heat was at first tolerable but as the sun rose overhead, the heat began to burn the little bird. By the time the sun set, the bird was dead.

There are three moral lessons to the story:
First, the one who puts you in the carabao dung need not be an enemy;
Second, the one who gets you out of the carabao dung need not be your friend; and
Third, when you are in it up to your neck, for heaven's sake, don't sing!

47

THE PARABLE OF THE TURTLES

Three turtles were strolling beside the river bank one day. They were the best of friends and enjoyed exchanging stories and recent happenings.

On the side was a nice clearing which was a favorite picnic spot among the townspeople. Children came to swim in the fresh water flowing from a spring in the mountain.

The three decided to stop at the picnic site. As luck would have it, they found an unopened bottle of softdrink.

"Wow!" one turtle exclaimed. "Let us have a picnic ourselves and drink to our health."

"Yes," agreed the other two. "Let us drink all of it."

But there was a slight problem. They could not find a bottle opener. So they looked at each other for some time trying to figure out how to open the precious bottle.

Finally, the biggest turtle said, "Let us draw lots. The one who gets the shortest stick must go home and get a bottle opener. Meanwhile, the two will wait here. How about that?"

They all agreed it was the only way to solve the problem. They drew lots and, by a stroke of luck, the littlest turtle drew the shortest stick. So he dutifully trudged towards his place to get a bottle opener.

In the meantime, the two turtles continued story-telling while waiting. After four weeks, the littlest turtle still had not come back. "Maybe he forgot or he might have met an accident. Or, worse, he might have been picked up by a human being."

The two turtles continued to wait, but after another two weeks they began to run out of stories. Not only were they hungry, they were also getting very impatient.

The biggest turtle grumbled. "Maybe he is not coming anymore. I have an idea. Let us break the capped part of the bottle with a stone. Some of the contents may spill out but there should be enough for us to drink."

"Excellent idea!" exclaimed his companion.

From a bush nearby, the littlest turtle shouted out, "If you do that, I won't go home to get the bottle opener!"

48

THE PARABLE OF THE BOAT

He was a typical individualistic farmer who did things according to his own judgment and lessons from past experience.

Reenforcement came from his neighbors. They called him *Piyok*, a term used for one who farmed alone. His farm was small so he needed no extra help. He owed no one any debt of gratitude and felt no need for reciprocity.

He managed somehow in his stand for complete independence and self-reliance.

One day, he took a boat ride across the river.

"Where are you going, Piyok?" the other passengers asked.

"To the other side to gather some firewood," he answered.

He sat on a piece of wood at the end of the boat. Now, while the boat was being rowed, Piyok fiddled with his bolo. Soon he poked the pointed end of his bolo and began to bore a hole on the base of the boat under him.

"Hey, Piyok, don't do that!" the other passengers shouted.

"This is my part of the boat," Piyok answered. "Leave me alone. Sit where you are and mind your own business. Do what you want and let me be."

He continued to wiggle his bolo on the base of the wooden boat. Suddenly, from the hole water spouted like a fountain. More and more water gushed inside the boat.

After a few minutes, the whole boat sank.

Even if Piyok was adamant in saying he only bored a hole on his part of the boat, the whole boat sank and with it all the people on board.

49

THE PARABLE OF THE FROG

The little frog was the butt of jokes and snide remarks. He was weak and could not do many things the bigger frogs performed with ease. Other frogs refused to let him join in their games. Even at home, his parents could not rely on him for chores and other household needs.

He was unhappy. But in time he learned to accept his fate, believing he was physically unfit.

As he grew a little bigger, he became known as the frog who could not jump. He felt disgraced, but again he accepted this as a reality of his sad life. He even noticed that his voice was too soft— hardly a croak worthy of a frog. When the rains came, all the other frogs would croak away merrily, while he kept quiet to himself, his voice barely a squeak.

One day, the little frog took a walk in the fields. His mind wandered. He thought of his misfortune and wondered what the future held for a weak frog who could not jump or croak. He even considered becoming some other animal—then he would not be expected to jump or croak. He would be normal, not looked down upon and despised and, worst of all, made fun of.

As random thoughts flitted through his head, he didn't notice a dry unused well nearby. Before he was aware of it, he fell into the hole ten feet deep. To complicate matters, the opening was grassy because it was an abandoned well.

No one would ever bother to look down, so who would save him? Jumping up was out of the question. He was the frog who could not jump—besides, the height was too much. Two feet high, maybe he could, but ten feet? Never!

He considered shouting, but his voice was so faint, no appreciable sound came out. His throat was also so dry with fear that even if he did manage a sound, no one would hear.

"I am dead," he said to himself, "that's for sure. Maybe I just should pray my last. Anyway, I am so unhappy up there, it is better to end my life. What good is a frog if he can't even jump and croak?"

While he was mulling over these thoughts, a big snake suddenly hissed from a few feet away. It was about to strike him. The neck of the snake widened, its head was raised and its tongue stuck out menacingly.

The little frog felt the danger and was taken aback. He could not believe what then happened. He burst into the loudest croak which made the snake retreat some. Then the little frog jerked his legs and catapulted himself high up in the air. It was as if an unseen spring had bounced him up all of ten feet and out of the empty well.

At last he realized that he was now a frog who could croak and jump!

50

THE PARABLE OF THE SNAKE

The frog hopped merrily on the soft soil drenched with rain. He enjoyed the forest best after a shower. The grass blades glistened with adherent globules of water. The breeze was pleasant to the skin. He croaked every now and then to express his joy at being alive.

He traced the tracks carefully, for occasionally, danger lurked around. A human being could trample him without warning. But he knew that when it rains men stay in their shelters. Still he listened carefully for any impending danger.

From afar, the frog saw a creature in its stillness. His sensor told him it was either a sleeping snake or one stealthily poised to attack. He stopped to retreat or go into the bushes. If it were a snake, it could snap him up and swallow him whole. That would be his end.

As the frog slowly swayed to make a jump onto the stalk of a reed nearby, the snake spoke. "Help me, please. I am wounded. A man struck me yesterday. I cannot slither for my body is crushed. If he had hit my head, I would have died. Fortunately, he only hit me with his cane on my trunk."

"I do not think I should," said the frog defensively. "Snakes eat us. We are told to avoid you, not help you."

"I know, but I am dying and too weak even to open my mouth at anything, let alone eat you. Please help me."

The frog took pity. In the dying state of the snake, the frog knew he was safe. He hopped nearer to check. True enough, blood was splattered all over its body, which was crushed almost in half.

Painstakingly, the frog pulled the snake along the path toward the brook. He and his family would be in a better position to nurse the snake back to health.

But his family and all the other frogs were shocked to see him pulling a snake. "What stupidity! You are consorting with the enemy. Let the snake die!" chorused the frog congregation.

"He is injured. The snake cannot harm us in his state of near-death. He is begging for help."

Still the others would not help, partly out of fear and mostly out of knowledge that many of their kinsfolk had perished in the mouth of snakes before.

The frog decided to do his act of mercy alone although his wife reluctantly assisted. They cleansed the wound and applied some salve. The sun took care of drying out the wound. Meanwhile, they fed the snake with what food was available.

In a week, the wound began to heal and in another fortnight, the snake could move with difficulty. The husband and wife frogs practically stayed with the snake all the time, attending to all its needs.

Day after day, the snake regained its strength.

"In a week more you will be fully recovered," said the mother frog. "Except for the scar on your skin and the slight curvature on your fractured backbone, you will be as good as new."

Because of the time spent together with the snake, all feelings of fear and doubt on the part of the couple frog disappeared.

Alas, on the day of his departure, the snake ate all the children of the frogs.

"But you said you will not eat us. Please do not do us any more harm," pleaded the father frog.

"That was when I was weak and dying. Now I am strong and hungry," proclaimed the haughty snake.

With that, it ate both the father and the mother frogs.

For he was a snake.

GLOSSARY OF PILIPINO TERMS AND PHRASES

Albularyo—herb doctor; herbalist
Alupihan—centipede
Araro—plow
Batang musmos—a very young person
Baul—footlocker
Bisita—to visit
Bisita iglesia—very brief visit to the chapel
Bobo—dull; stupid
Buri—palm
Camachili—a kind of fruit
Daga—mouse
Halaya—Purple yam jam
Harana—serenade
Hating kapatid—equitable division
Hindi ka na mabiro?—Can't you take a joke?
Hito—fresh water catfish
Inakay—featherless birdling
Ipanatag ang kalooban—Calm your feelings
Kabilang buhay—life beyond
Kamalig—rice bin; barn; warehouse; small granary
Kambal—twins
Kapilya—chapel
Konsehal—councilor
Konvento—convent
Kristo—cockfight bet-taker; matchmaker
Lambanog—distilled fermented coconut sap
Landas sa langit—way to heaven
Lechon baboy—roasted pig
Lechon manok—roasted chicken
Lubluban—carabao's wallowing hole
Macapuno—special coconut with thick meat
Malamangan—put one over on someone
Mano—kiss the hand as a sign of respect
Maong—blue jeans
Matandang kuluban—very old person
Matangos—high-bridged nose
Morkon—large home-made sausage

Nag-umpukan—clustered; crowd of people
Nakalimutan ang pinanggalingan—forgot one's origins
Ninong—godfather
Padre—priest; father
Pagpalain—bless; sanctify
Pagsasagawa—implementation
Pagtawid—to cross; to traverse a more direct route
Pancit—rice noodles
Pango—flat nose
Patron—patron saint; protector
Pinakabobo—dullest; most stupid
Pino o magaspang na asin—fine- or large-grained salt
Piyok—loner; individualist
Poong Maykapal—Lord; God
Puesto—stall; place for selling
Pusod—belly button; umbilicus
Putikan—mud puddle
Sabung—cockfight
Sabungan—cockpit; cockfight arena
Sa pula o sa puti—For the red or the white rooster
Selyo—stamp
Semana Santa—Holy Week
Takilyera—ticket dispenser
Tanga—stupid; fool
Tansan—soda pop cap
Tinikling—dance simulating a bird's movements using
                      bamboo poles
Topada—cockfight matches
Tuba—fermented coconut wine
Tutumbukin—directly in the path of; will hit right smack on
Utang—loan